Stop Running From God, Listen

By
Jose Sanchez

Editor
Lisa M. Williams
lmwilliams04@gmail.com

Dedication

This book is dedicated to God for being so supportive to me and helping me find solutions through most issues and obstacles that I have faced.

To my wife for her love, support and being the greatest instrument in helping me grow as a believer. You also helped me discover more about myself.
To Jesus Ventura, my parents, and the rest of my immediate and extended family, for whom I am grateful for. You inspire me to be better. To my nephew Beto Palacios for your detailed help with this book.

To my aunt Lisa Williams, thank you for your brilliant mind and strategic guidance with this project.

.

Table Of Contents

Preface

The purpose of this book is to help you start your process of drawing closer to God. For a large part of my life, I was distant from Him and this led me to screw up a lot. The idea for this book began around two years ago when it occurred to me that readers could benefit from my experiences.

There were several things that kept this book from being completed, like my own negative thinking. I also went through a period of just feeling physical burnout. I had worked in a detention facility for 11 years. During my last two years, I was physically and mental exhausted along with other coworkers.

I came across other factors that were discouraging. During my career transition, I experienced many challenges causing me to almost not complete this short book, but I kept realizing that God was putting it on my heart.

Intro

Life sucks feeling like God is so far away. Are you tired of wondering is God real? How do I know He is truly there? How can I know for sure He engages in my life? How is it possible to have a relationship with someone you can't see?

Like many people, I struggled with my relationship with God, most of my life. On occasions, wondered if He was with me, and if He really had my back. I remember times I was angry and cursed at Him because of negative circumstances I was subjected to.

Like any relationship, my road with God has been a long journey, full of mistakes and disappointments. If I would have practiced these principles earlier on in life, it would have saved me many heart aches.

This book will give you basic ideas on how to draw closer to the most powerful force in the universe. In addition, I'll point out topics such as, how to read the Bible, if He loves you, and other keys that will help you, not only draw closer to God, but also help you to continue to develop, and to be the better version of yourself.

..being justified by faith, we have peace with God through our Lord Jesus Christ.
By whom also we have access by faith into this grace, wherein we stand, and rejoice in hope of the glory of God.
Romans 5:1-2

Chapter 1
Don't blame God

When I was side swiped by a drunk driver years ago, which caused me to have three cracked ribs, it was not God's fault. The driver chose to drink alcohol and drive intoxicated. As I write this, I can recall I didn't even thank God that I survived the accident. As a matter of fact, at that time, I wasn't living right, and had also questioned my faith. After my accident, I unknowingly remained distant from God for years to come.

I remember for a good portion of my adulthood being resentful to my parents for dumb reasons, but when I let God in my heart, I spoke to Him about all those concerns and just gave it all to Him. Now I have a much better relationship with my folks. They are precious to me. The longer you wait to let go or resolve these past issues, the longer it strains your heart. I understand there are difficult things to forgive but it's an instrument of healing. Once you fire it off, the enemy can't control or redirect you anymore because the spiritual chains are broken.

You may have been through situations and blamed God for not preventing them from happening. I get it, even though, I don't know what you have been through. Here are my reasons why you can't blame Him:

1. God allows everyone to exercise their free will, good and bad.
2. When Eve and then Adam, took that first bite of the forbidden fruit that changed everything, the forces of darkness gained a certain authority over this world, and have continued to try to divide, confuse and discourage people ever since. If you doubt this just turn on the tv and try to find an episode that doesn't talk about ongoing violence, hate, racism, division of political views and communities. It wasn't God's fault I was exposed to representatives and members of the drug cartel business and criminal underworld. I believe it was the enemy trying to get me to commit to an entirely different life so that, inevitably, I would grow more distant from God, my Father.
3. This world is not perfect. The only thing perfect is God's love for us and the ability to embrace Him.

Chapter 2
Reach out to Him

"He says, 'Be still, and know that I am God.
I will be exalted among the nations,
I will be exalted in the earth.'"
Psalm 46:10
(NIV)

One of the things that drove me to that point was, that I got tired of making choices that still seemed to be followed by painful consequences. Apart from that, I did feel kind of screwed up. Another one of the big reasons was I could feel one of my kids emotionally drifting away from me. I just wanted to better myself in all areas, but I felt like I couldn't do it alone.

One day, I remember dropping on my knees and crying something to the effect of, " God! I'm tired of screwing up! I need your help! I need you in my life!!" A brief time later, I got baptized at the Chula Vista Marina (San Diego).

Since then, I have continued to pursue a better relationship with God. Don't get me wrong, I still have made plenty of mistakes since, but I try to learn from them. You're going to fail, fall short, and make mistakes. The more you focus on mistakes, resentment, and negativity, etc., the more it will continue to have power over you. The more you continue to reach out to God and focus on having a better relationship with Him, the more He will move in your life.

You have been the captain of your ship your whole life, look where it's gotten you. I'm not implying all readers have things wrong with them. I am directing my question to the readers that clearly are reading this book because of their flaws, past mistakes and, at a minimum, have a desire to better themselves, preferably having a desire to know God better.
Look, get off your behind and just do it! Tell Him in your words that you're sorry for all your wrongs and that you want Him in your life. That simple. Stop running from HIM!

Chapter 3

Read your Bible

Stop being complacent, read The Good Word. I always say it's the only way to learn the tactics and tricks of the enemy. This will also help you understand God better, and what some of His expectations are. I could get into that, but it would make the book longer. I certainly don't want to put you to sleep. Also, many people bled and died so that you can have that information available to you. You will discover that in the New Testament.

When I read the Word, I know God recognizes I'm trying to spend personal time with Him. I know that's got to count for something. Stop settling for a mediocre spiritual life, crack that book open and read it at least once a day. Just because you decided to be a Christian or you've been a believer all your life doesn't mean anything. Breaking news!! Satan can be a Christian and believer too. He's been in the presence of God on many occasions and infiltrated many Christian and religious organizations. He knows the Word front to back. He had to so that he can understand his enemy. He hates us! How do I know? Look at history.

117 - 138 AD

Around 117 to 138 AD the Roman kingdom eradicated several Jewish traditions in the holy land. Beginning with outlawing the Sabbath worship, festivals, circumcision, reading of the Tora (scriptures).

SPAIN

Subsequent of the Alhambra Decree in 1492, to end their effect on Spain's large 'converso' inhabitants and convinced its members not to revert to Judaism, many Jewish communities in Spain either converted or were banned and thrown out. In addition, in 1943 to 1945 ADOLF HITLER tried to completely wipe out God's people - the Jews.

Understand your enemy. He's been fighting all his life to make you feel distant and detached from God. That's one of his methods to make you lose faith. You must admit that at one time or another we have all felt that way. Take the time to recall how you dealt with feeling emotional isolation. Learning how to deal with these negative issues is important. Reading and spending time in the Word is a healthy spiritual habit that can also help you cope with life's issues and find the strength to persevere.

Chapter 4
How to read the Bible

There are many styles and perspectives on this. From 21-day devotional plans to reading a proverb a day. How well do you want to know God? How close do you want to draw to Him? My friend Emmitt Summers recommends you team up with a family member, or friend. Someone you love and or trust. He personally does a combination of the listed plans.

1 – BEGINNING TO END
My suggestion is to start from the beginning at the book of Genesis Chapter 1 verse 1. Daily read 1 to 3 chapters until you reach the end. Then start over. In the Old Testament He shows you how He tried to establish guidance, structure, and a relationship with His first, chosen people. in The New Testament He shows you how He approached establishing salvation for all people. Take your time, but if you're itching to understand salvation and Jesus better then indulge in the New Testament for now.

2 – ONE PSALM A DAY

This can be done independently or in conjunction with any other plan. There are over one hundred chapters in the book of psalm. The author was King David who continually expressed his faith and need for God.

3 – ONE PROVERB A DAY
This book was written by King Solomon, son of king David and includes thirty-one chapters. You will find that it offers reasons to trust and depend on God. You can do this alone or with another plan, regardless. Regardless, you will find this area encouraging. When you complete the book, you can start over again or alternate days.

4 - YouVersion
One of many mobile apps that offers hundreds of devotionals with audio and some videos. Helps you keep track of progress and schedule devotions and notifications. It also has issue specific content such as for marriage, dating, drug addictions, along with many more. You can have family and friends join you as well.

5 – Published Books
This should not replace reading the Bible. However, at some point it wil benefit you to find time to read books written by pastors, preachers, or evangelists. Good authors include Lee Strobel, R.C. Sproul, Joyce Meyers, etc. Do your research. Some may be more inspirational, others more scripture based.

Regardless of your preferred method, the idea is to begin to get familiar with His Word and establish a positive spiritual habit. This will improve your understanding of religion, God, Jesus, and most topics in the related area. Honestly, some people might feel confused and that's ok because there is so much information. Some is literal documented history and some are statements that are spoken in figurative meaning. Some read it and feel like they completely do not agree with God and things He allowed to occur. When this happens, it is important to address your issues with someone who has a clear understanding such as a pastor, minister, or bible study instructor.

FOR HE IS GOOD.
FOR HIS MERCY
ENDURETH FOREVER.
1CHRONICLES
16:34 KJV

Chapter 5
Quality time

COMMIT YOUR WAY TO THE LORD;
TRUST IN HIM,
AND HE WILL ACT
PSALM 37:5

In early 2021 I felt heart ache thinking about an unresolved issue with my 13-year-old son. He hadn't spoken to me in a year, over a verbal misunderstanding. This emotional pain was beginning to feel intolerable, again. I then went to my prayer area, opened up, and shared my concern with God. Then I waited in silence. During my quiet standby is when I started to feel His peace. I thanked Him for it. I had no doubt God saw me and heard my grief. I know it will be resolved, in His divine time.

I know it's easy to feel uncertain if God heard you or if He is even on your side. You should know that He hears, sees, and understands you. If He can place every star in its divine place in the universe, He can place all things in their respective place in your life, according to His will and timing. What helps me open up to Him is the faith I have that He is right there with me, listening.

Spending time with God is solely dependent on you. In any relationship, the key is to keep it healthy for both parties, and that it requires commitment, time, and communication.
Here are my suggestions. You decide what time and during the week works for you.

During the time I was working in a detention facility, I can recall often using #3. I can say while employed there, I never was assaulted or gassed, which is what happens when a detainee throws liquid with urine, and at times feces, in it. In addition, the private detention facility I used to work at didn't offer employees parking, or parking fee reimbursement. When I started to communicate with God more regularly, I noticed I wasn't struggling to find parking as much. I would arrive downtown and find parking very soon after. I would always thank God as soon as I found a spot.

1). BEFORE YOU BEGIN YOUR DAY
My routine is before I start my day, I read scriptures then talk to the Lord. Normally, I fast also. During this time, I give thanks, share my concerns, and lift up prayers. Randomly I give Him quiet time. It's during your session with God that it's important to turn off the TV and put away electronics. This has given me peace on many occasions even when I felt troubled or conflicted.

2). RIGHT BEFORE BED

This can be a suitable time for you especially because this offers an opportunity to put all the cares of the day aside, and just focus on God. Many types of relapses can occur at this time, which is why this might be a good exercise for those that it applies to. Especially if you suffer from nightmares this might be the routine for you. I can't guarantee specific results, but it's worth a try.

3). THROUGHOUT THE DAY

This method is good because it gives you an opportunity to include God and have Him in your thoughts throughout the day. While you're at work or in the middle of a drive you take the time to put everything aside to talk to God. Say hello and why you appreciate Him. While working in a jail, I would take a minute to stand in a corner out of everyone's view and just give thanks to God, and share other thoughts.

4). DURING FAMILY GATHERINGS

This is a wonderful time for family to share reasons why they are thankful and lift prayers and concerns to God together. The more that you pray, the less awkward you will feel if you are asked to lead in prayer. I heard it said once that, a family that prays together, stays together. For this reason, it is wise to include your spouse and kids.

5). IN YOUR HEAD

In general, I strongly recommend expressing your thoughts or prayers verbally. However, just as most of us have at some point allowed thoughts that are negative or self-destructive to settle in the back of our minds and allow them to grow to some extent, you can speak to God in your mind, where it is safe and no one can judge you or misunderstand you. I use this method most often while working in the detention facility.

6). COUPLES

In the morning, during the day or right before bed, this is a clever way for couples to redirect their thoughts to the Divine Creator as a single unit. With there being so many ways to have conflict and misunderstandings, this method of spending time with God can help to minimize conflicts.

What will help more is that you listen to each other uninterrupted, be receptive, and remember to share that you love each other no matter what is said or how it's said. Use low tones, respectful language and always acknowledge accomplishments, the positive side, or good attributes of your spouse. I'm no expert but I've learned the hard way, by experience. I have definitely upset my beautiful wife on many occasions. That could make for a wole separate book!

THE HEAVENS DECLARE THE GLORY OF GOD; AND THE FIRMAMENT
SHEWETH HIS HANDYWORK.
PSALMS
19:1 KJV

Chapter 6
Allocating time

"WITHOUT COMMITMENT YOU CANNOT HAVE DEPTH IN ANY RELATIONSHIP OR ANYTHING". NEIL STRAUSS

In the previous chapter, I addressed separate ways to approach your time with God. In this section, I want to stress the importance of being available for God. Look how far you came without Him holding your hand. Bathsheba and procreated with her while she was married to you Uriah the Hittite. not only did this lead to other sins or mistakes but this is proof of the condition of David heart during this time. He grew far from God and after he had achieved boundless success, material things of value, and several beautiful wives. He was too comfortable. Does that sound familiar? Tragic events followed which include his baby passing away. This grieved him. Emmitt Summers shared with me that, acquiring personal success without giving thanks to God often results in being humbled by God.

It's up to you on finding the time that fits well with you. One of the reasons I like to speak to Him in the morning is that I am still fasting. That's another form of commitment, to not even have a snack until I spend time with the Most Powerful Person in the Universe.

In our relationship we have come a long way. However, He has progressively helped me change attitudes and perspectives. This has helped me to be closer to my family. This is one of the most important aspects in obtaining and maintaining a connection with God. Look at it like this. If people can enjoy when you invest time in them, so does God. If people can appreciate when you do something for them, so does God. How do I know? Because HE is a person, a living, existing, full of energy, life, wisdom, and power beyond our understanding. He's alive, He's real, as real as the sun, moon and all the stars, and He put them there.

**DO NOT BE CONFORMED TO THIS WORLD, BUT BE TRANSFORMED BY THE RENEWAL OF YOUR MIND, THAT BY TESTING YOU MAY DISCERN WHAT IS THE WILL OF GOD, WHAT IS GOOD AND ACCEPTABLE AND PERFECT.
ROMANS 12:2**

Chapter 7

His presence

Even when I was lost in the world and communicating with people that were living a criminal life, I sensed God was near me. It's hard for me to explain, but if you have experienced a similar walk, you may understand. To this day, I am thankful that He allowed me to survive that road. The purpose of that feeling was to remind me to get out. No matter how difficult that would be He would be with me.

Only you have the power of convincing yourself that He is right there with you. Don't deny yourself this experience. One of the things I want you to try is when you're sitting down on a chair during this quiet session, I want you to picture Him standing next to you facing you. How does that make you feel? Take note. Here are other suggestions.

How do you feel His presence? With social media, Netflix, and music it's easy to be distracted and be completely disconnected with the most powerful source in the universe.

1. QUIET TIME: During your quiet time, you must silence your thoughts and emotions. The more you commit to this, the easier it will come. This can occur before or after prayer as well. Just be silent and block everything out. Trust that He is right there with you.

2. FAITH: I can tell you that He is with you during your prayer time, but if you don't have the faith, doubt sets in and it simply is not real to you. The Word says faith is a big aspect of our salvation. That is why, if you don't believe He is with you, loves and forgives you, then you give room to other negative thoughts and behaviors in your life. Such as addictions, resentment, neglecting loved ones and pushing others away.

3. BE CONSITENT: The more you practice my suggestions, the more you will naturally feel closer to God. If this is an area that you continue to struggle in, don't drop the ball. Speak to someone that is a professional in this area such as a pastor or preacher. Keep in mind, this can take time. Don't give up.

4. Practice positive affirmations such as:
A. I'm grateful God is with me, and for all the peace and blessings in my life.
B. I'm thankful for the relationship You (God) and I have with each other.

C. Get creative, reaffirm God's presence and place in your life. Reaffirm that you are a loving and forgiving person and that joy and resolve come naturally for you.

> *But God shows his love for us in that while we were still sinners, Christ died for us.*
> *Romans 5:8*

Chapter 8

Relying on God

But my God shall supply all your need according to his riches in glory by Christ Jesus. Now unto God and our Father be glory for ever and ever.
Amen.
Philippians
4:19-20

Relying on God means depending on and trusting in Him. Easier said than done. I find that often He allows circumstances in life so I can learn to come to Him. Often, I want to call one of my brothers to share and get their feedback. I believe God wants us to give Him that priority.

When Adam walked that heavenly garden, he could count on God to walk and hold discussions daily. When the new companion (Eve) came into the picture, the frequency of these discussions changed. The word is not clear about this, but Eve dropped the ball because she did not have the same relationship with God. Although this happened, God didn't destroy them on the spot. He clothed them and placed them somewhere else to begin their new lives.

Even though this occurred, God helped Adam live to the age of 930.

Moses led the Jews out of Egypt, he relied on God all the way to the Red Sea, where God parted it and drowned the pursuers. The story of Abraham is so symbolic on many levels. His journey represents our journey with God. During his journey, he messed up quite a few times but God was always with him. One of my favorite stories is about Joseph, son of Jacob. Joseph had eleven brothers that conspired to get rid of him permanently. They sold Joseph to passing merchants, unfortune continued to follow as he was also imprisoned for something he didn't do. The Bible never points out that he complained in any way. He stayed faithful in his belief in God and grew in wisdom and favor with others. Eventually he became second in command in Egypt. Through him God blessed and prospered his family because he relied on and had faith in God. In addition, he never compromised his integrity.

The more you rely on, and trust in God, the more He will lead you out of your place of isolation, despair, and release you from hopelessness and depression

Chapter 9
Be thankful

If people in satanic organizations can find things to be thankful for, so can we. If they can often verbally express reasons to give thanks to their higher arch of darkness, we should be able to do the same for the God of Israel. If nonbelievers can give daily thanks to the universe, we should be able to do the same for our Creator.

I have read several books and listened to audio books on personal development and success. More often this topic has a place in the content. When you genuinely feel thankful, people tend to notice in you a more positive attitude. I used to hate going to lunch first in the detention facility. Because I was thankful for my job one day, I decided to just get used to it. From then on, I went first. This also helped me to avoid conflict over the order. This was one of the reasons why some of the staff liked working with me. They knew they didn't have to go first. When you have a thankful and cheerful outlook, it becomes easier to adjust to, adapt to, and overcome challenges.

TODAY:
Find at least three reasons to express to God why you give Him thanks. Take the time to talk to Him and express gratitude. I know this may be challenging for some people, but you must continue to build and maintain that channel of communication

1. _____

2. _____

3. _____

JOURNAL:
You can provide a daily log of things you are thankful for in a journal.

REACH OUT:
You can call a family member, friend or accountability partner and identify things you are thankful for, or share from your journal. According to a Google search, the word "thankful" appears seventy-one times in the New Testament, and the concept of it comes up 102 times in the Old Testament. Write names of three people to reach out to.

1. _____

2. _____

3. _____

Many, O Lord my God, are thy wonderful works which thou hast done, and thy thoughts which are to us-ward: they cannot be reckoned up in order unto thee: if I would declare and speak of them, they are more than can be numbered.
Psalms 40:5 KJV

Chapter 10
He loves you

But God demonstrates his own love for us in this:
While we were still sinners, Christ died for us
Romans 5:8 NIV

This is an area I have struggled with for many years as I was growing up. Genuinely believing God loves me, despite my imperfections and flaws. At times, I felt I didn't matter to most people. These are attacks of the enemy. Scriptures clearly declare that we all matter to God. The only thing that keeps that space there is our thoughts and actions. I've said this before, be mindful of what you say to yourself in that area in your mind where it feels safe because no one can see that. That's also the area the enemy sends us negative messages so we can be discouraged from a powerful relationship with God. When we are discouraged from God, we unintentionally encourage others to be disconnected. Look at it like this: when we are happy and acknowledge God often, doesn't that encourage others to do the same? When we feel incomplete and have no relation with God, that, at times, has a similar effect.

I can try to convince you all day that God loves you, but what should occur is that you put effort to convince yourself. Figure out how to do that and if you're having trouble, this is common in our early stage of walking with God. Talk to someone that you are aware knows the Lord, whether it's a professional in ministry or someone that you can confide in.

This is how God showed his love among us: He sent his one and only Son into the world that we might live through him. This is love: not that we loved God, but that he loved us and sent his Son as an atoning sacrifice for our sins. Dear friends, since God so loved us, we also ought to love one another
1 John 4:9-11 NIV

Chapter 11

Pray for others

Praying always with all prayer and supplication in the Spirit, and watching thereunto with all perseverance and supplication for all saints. Ephesians 6:18 KJV

One of the reasons God directs us to pray for others is because this is part of being a community. Also, we are under constant spiritual attacks and it's our prayer intersessions that help to make positive changes and shifts in the spiritual realm.

When you turn on the TV, it is evident how dominant the influence of the enemy is on our world and our global economy. The fingerprints of the enemy are hate, violence, division, discord, confusion, calamities, and scandals. Satanic organizations are committedly praying for communities on a global scale, to be subjected to all these evil spiritual attacks. If they practice this level of commitment, including fasting, we should be able to do the same thing, supporting and praying over each other in the name of Jesus. Declaring healing, resolve, family unity, and divine protection, breakthroughs, and salvation.

You never know what someone is going through. That person that cuts you off on the freeway might be having a difficult day because they lost their job. That representative that hangs up on you might be having a near anxiety attack because she's having serious issues with her husband.

I remember a lady I used to work with years ago. She didn't believe in God, always complained, and criticized others. I heard a few years later that she got cancer. If people would take the time to let go and release all their negative energy and pray for others, this would be a much better and happier place. Listen, in Matthew 5:44 Jesus tells us to pray for our enemies. Now I'm not saying if everyone prayed this would be a perfect place or there would be no illnesses, and no problems. Put simply, it would be a better place. Praying and relating with each other makes for a better community also.

Chapter 12
Do not fear the enemy

For God hath not given us the spirit of fear; but of power, and of love, and of a sound mind.
2 Timothy 1:7 KJV

We will always be at war with the enemy. Aside from God, Christian communities, and families, there are angelic forces always trying to intercede. The point is you are never alone. Some of the enemies' tactics include causing you to feel stranded, isolated, suicidal, and spiritually or emotionally off-track. During this type of season, the enemy can bombard you with thoughts, such as feeling unvalued, hopeless, rejected, abandoned, unloved or depressed. One way to summarize how they are all related is that they are negative thoughts and can be extremely self-destructive. Prior to and during these challenges is when it is ideal to place focus on God and exercise our spiritual habits. This type of implementation not only will assist with continuing to help you grow your relationship with the most powerful source in the universe but it will also allow those spiritual attacks to be ineffective against you.

When we allow these attacks to be untreated, we surrender our peace of mind, faith, and ability to maintain a sound mind. Sounds crazy? It's the type of thing that I wish we learned in school to help us prepare for supernatural warfare. I, like many folks, grew up in a Catholic home where I was taught prayers and was made aware that God and the devil exist. I was also taught to also include that the only way to deal with these forces is to "be good."

I thank God that during my short dark journey as a youth I didn't end up incarcerated or dead. At the time, I was unaware that I was under attack from the prevalent, existence and influence from Satan and his unseen assistants or demons. This was one of the scariest times of my life. When you fail to recognize the variety of red flags, such as a friendly warning from a friend, a dream, encounters with law enforcement, including the FBI, well, if you don't change course, there can be serious consequences. The most profound one is death because in this place, you no longer can exercise your free will, encourage others, or encounter spiritual growth. One of the most unfortunate results is that in death, you cease to experience drawing closer to God.

Chapter 13
Do a self-check

It is important to take the time to be self-aware, of your thoughts and feelings. What are you whispering to yourself when no one is looking? I've heard a saying, "it is normal for birds to hover over your head, just don't let them nest there."

The enemy is an expert at sending you negative thoughts to discourage you from sharing time with God. This is an advanced strategy of the enemy because the more he succeeds in this type of attack, the less we inspire, encourage each other, and grow in the ways of God.

I don't have a degree in this field, but despite my daily study of the Word, I have been battling with the enemy since I was a child. Aside from having menacing dreams as a child, I have seen and heard threatening voices as a kid that were traumatic at the time. Something I still recall, clearly.

If you're having trouble identifying areas, talk to someone that knows you well. At times, during a discussion with my brother, German, he will share things to point out where it appears I'm at mentally. The funny thing is he

9

often does it even if I'm not asking for that type of feedback. Instead of me reacting defensibly, I just listen and try to recognize how that applies to me. More often, I find it helpful and that's one of the reasons I appreciate our relationship because he is very candid and genuine.

Taking Ownership

When you take the time to be aware of your thoughts and negative self-talk, this can make it a little easier to take ownership for our mistakes. When people hear you take ownership for misdeeds, not only can this help to restore respect and bring resolve, but it will also help minimize the negative thing you might tell yourself.

Don't let it go

When you become aware that you have overstepped your boundaries, made a serious mistake, hurt someone else, it is critical that you take action to bring resolve. Don't let these types of actions just slip away untreated. In my opinion, the best form of treatment is to allow the other party to know that you are regretful for your actions and ask for forgiveness. Often people don't even need to hear an explanation or a reason why you did what you did. However, if you feel it's appropriate, one approach can be, "at the time, "and add your explanation. Be careful because sometimes people can interpret your reasons as you trying to justify your actions. Remember, taking ownership is ofter more important than your side of the story. Use your best judgment.

Chapter 14

Common Mistakes

Not taking the time to meet with God

It's quite easy to put this time off. That's why I also recommend talking to Him in your head. It's easy and you can do this when you're in the restroom or on the road.

Being too super fired up

I have known people that in their beginning phase, they dictate to others all these things they need to know to be right, be saved and know God. Often, this is a horrible approach and tends to turn others off. I was there, too, and accused of being too preachy and too religious. During your walk, you need to remember that your primary purpose is to have and maintain a relationship with God. You're not here to convert others, especially in a time when you're just starting to learn and grow in God.

Too religious

Some leaders out there will expect you to fast because they do. Pray for 5 hours a day because they do. Go to church 4 days a week because they do. Pray a certain way because they do. Use certain garments during prayer because they do. This is excellent for individuals that have a relationship with God in this manner. However, what I suggest you focus on, for now, is to be available for

God daily and discover how to do it best. Also, important to recognize the areas you need to work on, the very first should be to learn to acknowledge to God your sins or issues, and ask Him to help you. Baby steps.

Not working on a relationship with God
This is one of my biggest regrets. I wish, I could go back and do this. I am so fortunate that I didn't get myself killed and I didn't put myself in a situation to seriously hurt someone else. Another way to look at this is if you don't take the time to work on your relationship with God, this is selfish. When I was at fault, I was clearly was giving priority to doing what satisfied my flesh and often in a sinful way. Along the way, I caused a few disappointments and broken hearts.

Not Being Honest
I'm not promoting harmless lies, but could it depend on the circumstance? There are those that may argue that it's not a big deal that you lie to your spouse about liking the dinner she put together when you didn't really enjoy it. Others will declare that it's a big time no-no. Use your best judgment, but always be honest with your spouse, but don't be negative, discouraging, unappreciative or brutal.

I will present to you that if you can't be honest with yourself about you, this is one of the biggest types of cancers that can lead to other more serious issues. This is also a common trait with people that are narcissist or addicts. You have to be able to look at yourself in the mirror and identify faults and areas to work on.

Easily Discouraged

This commonly occurs when we set unreasonable expectations for ourselves or others. If you're telling God you're going to start going to church or hoping that He will change something about your spouse or loved one, don't get discouraged if they don't change. You can't force people to follow you or God. The best lesson you can give others is to live by example and be patient. Instead of worrying about their progress, focus on yours. Especially in a marriage, you're not there to teach and instruct your spouse. Your sole purpose is to love and support them. If you're having serious issues in your marriage, for example, your spouse is a drug addict or gambling addict, you can read material that promotes how to deal with these issues. You can also speak to a counselor, therapist, or fellow clergy member.

Lack of Support

Scripture says to not forsake fellowship of the brethren. Not forsaking the assembling of ourselves together, as the manner of some is but exhorting one another: and so much the more, as ye see the day approaching Hebrews 10:25

God is telling us if we allow ourselves to meet with other believers this can be very spiritually beneficial.

Iron sharpens iron, and one man sharpens the face of his neighbor. Proverbs 27:17

Not only does this help give us a sense of community but can provide a platform for support and prayer intersession. Church, bible studies and other local/supportive gatherings can also provide information on other helpful resources that might apply to you. Also, if you're dealing with a serious issue like drug addiction, it would be beneficial for you to commit to a N.A. meeting.

Not Committed
Professional athletes don't reach success overnight. Having an official relationship with God requires your personal time, commitment, and communication with HIM. One of the reasons I try to stay on track is this is another method that helps me be the better version of myself. I feel like I have an obligation to be the better version of myself for God, my sake, and my family. In your journal, I want you to share why a relationship with God is so important. I want you to include areas on which you must focus.

Overwhelmed

When you're setting goals for yourself, it's ok to indicate several, but I want you to narrow it down to seven goals. From there, I want you to work on one at a time. You can work on more than one at a time, but I want you to keep it simple and not overwhelm yourself.

Perhaps take one to two weeks (or even 21 days) to focus on one goal. You can manage the approach but keep it simple, in the method that helps you stay in the game.

Failure

In this process, there is no failure, only lessons. When you have slip ups don't be hard on yourself. Rather, get back in the ring and fight! We all make mistakes but the more you focus on them the more you live there. You're not a failure, you're not a mistake. You're a highly favored child of God. You just need to convince yourself.

Celebrate

As you go along in this journey, take the time to recognize and even celebrate small victories. Treat yourself to a movie or dinner. This might sound funny, but when you recognize and allow other to celebrate your victories with you, this also helps to reaffirm community and feel support. In this process, you might encourage someone to overcome their challenges and ask you for feedback.

Chapter 15
Triggers

Triggers can lead to relapse and the gravity is dependent on your specific issues. Relapses can influence many to drift from God, so be mindful on what your triggers are. On your journal, it might help to write down what your triggers are and identify what things you can do to prevent or offset them. For example, if you know hanging out with Jim usually results in getting drunk off your rear, then, stop hanging out with him. If hanging out with Melissa causes you to have adulterous desires, then cut that off.

It's your world, and if you don't take charge of it in a positive manner the results can be catastrophic. I've been there, and like you, I have battled with many demons throughout my life and have made many mistakes. Mistakes give you something to learn from. If you don't learn from them, they can eventually be repeated.

Road rage
When I was much younger, I had a road rage incident and flashed my magic finger at the other driver. I was reacting to the driver giving me a look as he passed me

up. We both pulled over on the freeway and proceeded to get out of our vehicles. When we walked up to each other I realized he looked like a retired police officer and was behaving like he was hiding a gun behind him. Naturally, that concerned me and didn't want to escalate the situation any further so I proceeded to return to my vehicle. As I did this, he began to yell obscenities at me. If this would have occurred at an earlier time in my life, it would have ended much differently for him, or for me as well. One of my triggers has always been disrespect. Fortunately, I recognized the potential danger and chose to walk away.

Loud Voices

During the time that I have been married, I have learned to recognize that when my wife and I get into heated discussions, she can get a little bit loud. When she has raised her voice at me, there have been times I chose to walk away and go for a walk to allow things to de-escalate. Sometimes this angers her more because she prefers for us to continue to and finalize our discussion. I often try to tell her on my way out, "babe, I love you but, I need to calm down, when I get back, we'll work this out." Don't ever just walk away and slam the door shut because this is aggressive behavior and can cause things to escalate.

Bedtime

A friend of mine had mentioned that he would tend to have a certain relapse at bedtime. This is normally the time when people are tired and have time to let their mind wonder. One suggestion I gave him was to put on some worship music or an audio reading of scriptures. If you have a similar issue, get creative and try to come up with something to help you deal with your specific issue. If you can't produce a solution talk to someone you trust, like an accountability partner or professional in the medical field.

Chapter 16
12 Declarations to Recovery

Before you continue, please note that this chapter and all other section of this book are not intended to replace any official programs designed for persons with addictions. I want to remind you that I am not a medical professional and not qualified to promote or critique official 12-step method or programs. Rather, look at it as a friend sharing his perspectives.

Declare the power you have over your life: This God given power is the ability to choose for and commit to yourself. Exercise this power with positive affirmations that affirm this to be true.

1. God is with me and helps me be the better version of myself
2. My heart and mind are aligned with the love of God
3. I am thankful for my unlimited faith and healing
4. I'm open and transparent with other
5. Even though I am not perfect, I am created by a perfect God
6. I am open to receive God daily and full of the Holy Spirit

7. I am receptive to God and give him access to remove all resentment and negativity.
8. I own up to my errors and always apologize with ease.
9. I am a child of God and easily bring conflicts to resolve
10. I live in humility and draw closer to God daily.
11. I seek God often and appreciate the joy, blessings, and favor in my life
12. Accept the things I cannot change, pray for strength to continue change for the better.

If you feel these don't apply to you, take charge and be creative. Compose your own list. My goal is to encourage, inspire and point you to a positive direction. In the end, you are the driver of your own wheel. If you change your list, make sure you have it noted in your journal or somewhere you can refer to.

Chapter 17
Trust God

Trusting God comes down to what you think and tell yourself. Even though I touched on this in previous chapters, I want to focus more on it here. What is your level of trust in God? If you struggle with it, why is it? It would be good if you can make note of your answers in your journal. Presently exists a multitude of things that are tough to answer, and there are things we will never know.

My wife couldn't believe me when I told her yesterday on our drive home from Fontana, California that 91 percent of ocean life has still not been discovered. My point to her was despite our advanced technology, there is still a lot we do not know. When I looked it up, I discovered an article that said that more than 80 percent of our ocean is unmapped and unexplored. The same can be said about your relationship with God and your potential. They are tied together, hand in hand, because our choices can drastically vary based on our relationship with God.

Please don't compare how others display their relationship with God to the way yours is. Sometimes this helps us establish a level we might want to achieve. Just don't shoot too high. Like the saying goes, you must learn to crawl before you can walk.

There was a pastor I used to look up to. This man would give exceptional Bible teachings during church service. One day during service he confessed to the congregation that he had committed adultery. The leaders had asked him to stand down from the pulpit for a brief period and he refused. Shortly after he started a separate church. In 2011 he committed suicide due to being under investigation for fraudulent loans.

The point to the story is that sometimes the people you admire and want to look up to really might not have it all together. At a minimum, no one is perfect. I believe when Covid started, this period helped my trust in God build on a whole other level. Not only did my wife and I start to draw closer to each other but she started to cook more as well. Oh my God, n the present time she cooks so good and so much better. Her rice, cakes, pies, tacos, burritos, avocado toast, grilled cheese sandwich, chili dogs. She is a phenomenal cock and wife. She was already a good person but she has evolved to such a sweet loving wife and much more affectionate. I thank God for her many positive changes and for the many blessings along the way. Even though I have experienced many blessings and victories, I have also experienced many challenges and pain. With those difficulties I trust God that eventually they will be worked out. You can't make deals with God and set conditions that you will be receptive to Him if your son decides to finally open the channel of communication. You can't say, well if my daughter stops running around on the streets, I will serve you. In my experience, HE doesn't work like that. Those are also examples of unreasonable expectations. You try that approach you might just be setting yourself up for disappointment.

Challenge
I challenge you to do this: write down five goals you would like to achieve within the next two years. For example:
1. Acquire a business loan,
2. Author a book on your life
3. Be a more initiative-taking spouse
4. Attend church more regularly
5. Community outreach

List your five ideas below

1. _____

2. _____

3. _____

4. _____

5. _____

The reason for this is as you grow in your relationship
with God and pray over these goals, keep track of your
accomplishments. Sometimes life can get in the way of
our goals and sometimes we change our goals. What
should remain consistent is your relationship with God.
The more you commit to it, the more you will grow to
completely trust God.

How do I trust Him?
When you talk to God, don't try to understand Him and
don't expect the answer to come to you immediately.
When you are in prayer, don't overthink what you say or
what He will think. Stop telling yourself that you spoke
too much or you didn't pray long enough. What's keeping
you from totally trusting God is your doubt and your
doubt is affected by your thoughts. Just as you can trust
your parent to be supportive, coworker to be helpful and
a Walmart associate to help you out, know that God can
hear your concerns, thoughts and He loves you. If you're
not sold on this just yet, it's all good, most things take
time. Lift them prayers up, let yourself love and let it go
in God's hands. Someone told me recently: "Let God, and
let go."

Before you do a google search, let me ask you a question. What are things you can begin to do to truly feel you trust God? I implore you to write them down in your notes or personal journal. I want you to list as many as you can. I just had an idea. If you share with me your ideas, perhaps I can include them in a future book. That sounds exciting. Now if you go running off with my idea and write your own book at least give me a little credit.

Chapter 18
Love God

Beloved, if God so loved us, we also ought to love one another
1 john 4:11

When you love God, you want to spend time with Him. It makes it easier to trust and confide in Him. When you love God, you have Him in mind more often. I read an article on this topic that said if you want to love God, follow the ten commandments. I completely disagree. That's like someone telling you that you need to be faithful to your spouse. When you love someone, the commitment is automatic. No one needs to demand it from you.

Love others
We cannot build healthy relationships with our Divine Creator if we go around hating other people. Make yourself available for a friend or coworker. Sometimes lending someone an ear can go a long way. I know this isn't easy, especially for people that are not supportive of you. In the past, I have dealt with individuals that not only weren't supportive, but I was aware they were

talking trash about me. I can author a whole other book about these people. When these negative feeling arise about them, I try my best to pray over this and ask God to remove these negative thoughts from me. There have been times when this was a lot more challenging, but I try my best.

Love your family
Primarily, you should love your parents. If your relationship with your family is estranged, it would be wise to make things right. If you find yourself complaining and saying negative things about them, cut it out. These are indicators that you need to resolve your issues. The more you love others and your family, the better for your relationship with God. Sometimes to let go, we need to forgive, and I know this isn't always easy.

Love your wife (spouse)
I have said that your relationship with your wife, reflects your relationship with God. If you find yourself complaining about her, stop it and try to work things out. At least begin to be aware that you do this and how often. I'm no exception, in the beginning, I would find things to complain about her. As I started to grow in my relationship with God, one day, it just came to me. My purpose with her is not to teach and correct her, but only to love her, support her and accept her completely for who she is. Now if you are having serious issues in your

relationship, consider speaking with a professional. The less you complain about your soul mate, the less others can find to criticize about you. Here is a list of some things that can occur if you continue with this bad habit.

List of consequences

1. Gossip spreads about you
2. Your wife can find out and be hurt or devastated
3. You begin to lose interest in her
4. You begin to depreciate her
5. The other woman you share with starts acquiring the tools to slowly manipulate you in thinking she is the better alternative.
6. You become more miserable or depressed
7. Gives others the impression you lack integrity
8. Gives others impression you are a poor decision maker

There are many articles that list all these things you must do to grow your relationship with God. You really don't "have to" do anything. Just as you naturally want to support those you love and be present for them, the same applies with God. You don't have to go to the gym, but countless people do to take care of their bodies. You don't have to support your wife but you do because you love her. You don't have to love God, but loads of people do, and as a result, help with outreaches, attend worship gatherings, and assist in other community areas. For the love of God, some people leave their families to become missionaries in other countries and learn a new language. I'm not asking you to do anything. At a minimum, continue your commitment of being available and talk to Him. You build any relationship with time, communication, and trust. Be patient on your approach with God.

Some will say if you don't go to church, speak in tongues, not filled with the Holy Spirit, you don't love God and you're not saved. No one has the authority to tell you the latter. Yes, these are awesome things to have in your life but just focus on your relationship. There's no rules, no deadlines, no signatures, or mandatory exercises. Only thing God would like, is you start making time for Him. He misses you and would like to hear from you. Be it in church, your closet, or living room floor.

Chapter 19

Church Resources

It is possible that some churches don't have as many resources as others. However, here is a list that most provide, especially in my area.

- Ministries for food distribution
- Life classes or life groups
- Community events
- Men,
- Women
- Children
- Sports
- Finance
- Business
- Prayer
- Cooking
- Arts and crafts
- Street evangelism

Chapter 20
Additional Resources
(San Diego, Ca)

Resources below are for those that it might apply. You can also dial 211 for additional information.

Affordable housing assistance
San Diego Housing Commission at 619-231-9400

Emergency Food Pantry
Sustaining Grace Outreach Center Inc.
Provides an emergency food pantry for those in need.
(619) 401-4006

Emergency Food Pantry, CCSA Clairemont Center
Community Christian Service Agency
Provides emergency services to low-income individuals and families. Emergency food is available up to six times per year
(858) 274-2273

Light for Life Foundation

Provides young people with knowledge to increase help seeking behavior for themselves or on behalf of others.
Eligibility
www.yellowribbonsd.org
(760) 635-5904

National Suicide Prevention Lifeline

Provides free and confidential emotional support to people in suicidal crisis or emotional distress.
Eligibility
(800) 273-8255

Free or low-cost counseling
https://www.opencounseling.com/california/san-diego

Youth crisis support (California)
https://calyouth org/cycl/

Chapter 21
International Resources

For more relevant information on your needs, Google search or contact your local resource center.

R.I International
For crisis, outpatient, housing, community support teams, and more. https://riinternational.com/

United For Mental Health
For mental health support and aiding organizations in policy, global information, and financing. https://unitedgmh.org/mental-health-support

National Alliance on Mental Illness
Suicide awareness and global resources https://www.nami.org/Home

Global Foodbank Network
For food, worldwide resources, and donations https://www.foodbanking.org/

Marriage coaching
https://www.poweroftwomarriage.com/info/free-online-marriage-counselirg/

Smart Recovery
Global addiction support resources and online tool
https://www.smartrecovery.org/

Chapter 22
Closing Thoughts

You must be patient because this road is not easy. It can be difficult to face any challenge alone. That's one of the reasons it will benefit you to draw closer to God. Even though this can be tough in the beginning, I urge you to never give up. Take advantage of your local support groups in your community so you can grow with others, establish accountability partners, and have an outlet.

Don't waste time arguing with others about the right way to approach this or what others need to focus on. Just focus on staying committed to your relationship with God and your personal growth.

Lastly, I can't thank my wife Monica Sanchez enough for being supportive, and for being there in my stressful moments. Her loving nature, beautiful smile and laughter always made things better.

I truly hope you enjoyed this small book. Feel free to share your questions and progress on my social media @XTRNL619

About the Author

I was born in Yuma, Az in 1973 to two parents from San Luis, Mexico. I've had a few hobbies since I was a kid but writing seemed to stick with me the longest, from publishing rap music and then my first book on the Keto Diet in April 2020 (also available on Audible).

Prior to my eleven-year tenure in a detention facility as an officer, I established over fifteen years in the transportation area. I began with school buses and then with a private company in public transit.

No matter what line of work I was in, I always had a passion for helping others. Before Covid19 I had the privilege on several occasions, where I assisted in public outreaches with my friend Jesus Ventura. During these outreaches, we enjoyed handing out clothes, food, and many prayers to the homeless community.

At this time, I am working on a book that is fiction but shares many events inspired by my life. My goal is to get it on the big screen, such as Netflix, so a broader audience can be impacted in a positive way.

My hope is that my readers will experience much personal growth along with a deeper relationship with God.

So, whether you eat or drink, or whatever you do, do all to the glory of God first
Corinthians 10:31

Book Recommendations

The Mate Wait
(Christian Novel)
By Lisa M Williams
Lmwilliams04@gmail.com

The Case for a Creator
(Christian/Fiction)
By Lee Strobel

Battlefield of the mind:
Winning the battle of your mind
(Christian/Self-Help)
By Joyce Meyer

"FOR TRULY, I SAY TO YOU, IF YOU HAVE FAITH LIKE A GRAIN OF MUSTARD
SEED, YOU WILL SAY TO THIS MOUNTAIN, 'MOVE FROM HERE TO THERE,' AND
IT WILL MOVE, AND NOTHING WILL BE IMPOSSIBLE FOR YOU."
MATTHEW
17:20 ES